SCREAM

until you know what God is

by Liz Bajjalieh

Fernwood
PRESS

SCREAM until you know what God is

Fernwood Press
Newberg, Oregon
www.fernwoodpress.com

Printed in the United States of America

Cover and page design: Mareesa Fawver Moss
Cover art: Liz Bajjalieh
Author photo: Richard Bajjalieh

ISBN 978-1-59498-223-1

For Grandpa Naim,
I'm sorry I never had the privilege of getting to know you.
But please know, forever, that I love you.

Contents

If God's not dead, what is she?

A note on pronouns:

This text uses pronouns for God outside of he/him, and this not only includes she/her/hers and they/them/theirs, but neopronouns such as zi/zim/zir, xe/xir/xirs, and fae/faer/faers.

Neopronouns are pronouns typically used by some nonbinary/transgender people to express their gender. According to The Trevor Project, about 4 percent of LGBT youth today use neopronouns.

If you see zi/zim/zir, xe/xer/xyrs, or fae/faer/faers in the text and aren't sure what they mean, they are pronouns. These sets are just a few examples of many neopronouns: as we better understand ourselves as individuals and as gender evolves/returns to definitions stolen from us by colonization, so does the language we use to describe it.

1. God is
A web of lies
And we are stuck
At the center

2. God is the horizon
At dusk, the dividing line
Between where the day takes its leave
And the night cycles in
The shivering hours of the unknown

3. God is a canoe
Floating down a foggy river
Just keep paddling

And paddling

And paddling

And paddling

4. God sleeps like a dead tree
Rolled over in wet dirt
Where the forest canopy blocks out the sun

Without the light from above
Their eyes fall thick into a drowse

They sink further into the mud
Until they, too, are the earth

5. God bleats like a sheep
Calling from a mountain too high
I try to call back

But she cannot hear me
I wonder if
She'd ever heard me, anyway

6. God is a book
With a cover
Bent too far back

7. God is a game you can't win
A hill you'll never climb
A tower you wish you'd never built

8. God is something
We can't name
God is something
We can only take

9. God is a crooked path
Meandering through a looking glass

10. God drips from my hands
Like water from a shower
It starts from my head
Arches down my neck, shoulders, arms
To the tips of my fingers
Before dribbling down the drain

11. God is a skyline of skyscrapers at night
Swaying in the dim of my tired eyes

Each building has a soul of their own
And carries our dreams higher
Than we ever could

12. God sleeps
Between bridges
On the Potomac River
Facing Virginia, the water keeps her warm

13. God is tatreez
Embroidery stitched by stubby fingers
Forming pink diamond roses
Golden cypress leaves
And red apple branches

The artist knows
That life lives between
The needle and the thread

14. God has no truth
Clasped between her hands
Only tales as high as harvest corn
But as weak as her brittle, old bones

15. God is a line
Of your novel

That you hope

Doesn't fall over

The edge

Of the page

⊙ ⊙

16. God holds my hand
At the new town movie plaza
His knuckles tense but electrified

Like a mother
I hold on, too
Tenderly cradling
The poor hope
That lives between his fingers

17. God aches for their father
As they lie across their bed

While he sleeps just down the hall
The man is miles away

18. God spins like a carousel
Barefoot on a field, wheeling with a smile
All around them, the many shades
Of our rich blue sky
Bleed into one

19. God squeaks like the floorboards
A timid love shies away from the sound
As she makes her way to the door

⊙ ⊙

20. God is candied apples
A taste of ecstasy
That breaks your teeth
When you take a bite

21. God is
A coupon
The miracle
Of three dollars off
Your next bottle
Of hair conditioner

Reaching through
Your unkempt purse,
You found it
Right as
Your former
Sea breeze
Scented savior
Ran dry

For a moment
You are
A pastor of finance
A prophet
For smart shoppers everywhere
And the blessed ink
On the thermal paper
Is the sacred text of your new Bible

22. God is dandruff
Covering a white bed sheet
You don't see him
But you *feel* him

⁂

23. God is a single string
Woven into a blanket
Where you and I can sleep

24. God dances under my skin
Causing goosebumps
A stiff neck
And a sideways back

25. God is a tune
That sings from my veins
A melody like a velvety remedy
A vibrancy to cast out the impurities
Hiding in the crevices of me
So I can be free
From this stiff and rigid body

26. God pulsates through your bloodstream
Like a parasite
Swimming toward your center
Gashing through your lungs
Gnawing at your ribs

My Lord,
You whimper
Please stop
You're cutting through what's left of me

But she continues
Ignoring your pleas
Her mouth deep
Within your probiotic gut

27. God is a wool jacket
Saving me from bitter winter chills
But thanks to my allergies
Also giving me a slight rash

28. I sat next to God
On a bed made of twine
There was a bird on the window
And a banjo in my hands

Fae sang me a song
As sweet as summer heat
And I played faer a lullaby
To help faer fall asleep

29. God is a love
Soaked in rainwater
Then covered by a blanket
Until they are dry

30. God is sweet lemon tea
Poured from a broken pitcher
Beads of sweat drip down its sides
While the sun beats through the center

31. God is a song
Sung too many times
By a child on a creaking rocking chair
Back and forth
Back and forth
The mother yearns for silence

32. God is melting
Between the buttons of my keyboard
Oozing into the hard drive
Sizzling my poor baby's memory chip

33. God lives
Between the notches of my spine
Xe told me that there's a child
Who hopes to rest between my ears
I told xyr that's just fine
As long as the kid pays rent on time

34. A bell springs from God's shoulders
Clinking, clanging
A holy cacophony echoes through the sky

A well-suited man
Walks beneath his feet
And shouts, chest to throat,
Turn that shit DOWN

35. Time is wild
But God sits at its center
Smoking a joint
He lifts his glass to the moment
Cheers, mate

Of course, no one hears him
He sighs, flicking his ash to the ground

36. God is alone
Fae stares out onto a barren field
Heavy below the dry sky
Fae wonders if this cloudless blue will ever go away

37. God smells
Like fresh raspberries
Crushed by feet
That were cleaned in a crisp river

If you could
You'd pack their jammed berries into jars
And leave them by the salt in your cabinet
Hoping to remember them
For your whole wheat toast

38. God is
That feeling you get
On the edge of your arms
When you bend them toward the sky

Your heart is full
Your face sleeps
Into an easy smile

39. God is the woman who dances in my head
Ze stretches between the pews
In a flowing black dress
That falls right above zir knees
No shoes, only bare feet, bare legs
Daring to cast themselves toward the sky

40. God leaps from my heart
With glitter in her eyes
New sneakers on her feet
And legs ready to run

Praised be the God
That lives within us all
Even when she leaves
For a journey of her own

41. God waters my garden
Until it's overgrown
Hydrangeas crawling past the fence
Cherry trees casting suburban shadows
That cool our quiet bungalow

Cucumbers so heavy
Their weight pulls them from the vine
Until they roll onto the sidewalk

My only hope
Is that the neighbors don't trip!

42. God is a closet packed with vintage blazers
The doors are open wide, the sleeves rippling out like waves
Neon, flowered, a 1980s dream
So full of pounding personality
You can almost hear them scream

43. God is a rubber adhesive
A woeful duct-tape residue
Blocking the view through the window

You try to scratch him off to see fresh snow
Glistening in the moonlit street

44. God plays another tune for my sweet summer head
Rhythms that crunch like fall leaves
Chords that bristle like winter wind
Lyrics that seep like spring rain into the soil

45. God whispers
Their thoughts
Into my ears
While I sleep

Someday
I'll remember
To write down
Their words

46. God will carry your burdens
But not if they're too sticky
He doesn't like getting stuff stuck on his hands

47. God keeps eating out of the trash can
Why does xe do that?
There's perfectly good food on the table

48. God is a breath
Of clean air
On the mountainside
So many of us
Dream of such joy
Yet rarely
Can most of us live it

49. God is a burden
Heavy in my arms
I just want to drop him
Like a mother might a child

But I can't
He clings so fiercely
That he's ripping through my skin

50. God lies on the floor
Arms and legs spread wide
Much like the stars she created

51. God is a pulse
God is stagnant

God rages
Like electricity

God is still
Let them rest

52. God is a Styrofoam cup
Left on the street
Crushed by commuter feet

You'd think he'd be sad
Forlorn on the cracked pavement
But how can a piece of trash
Something so material, soulless
Bereft of thought, feel a damn thing?

53. There are no answers
For whom
Or for what
God happens to be

Calm down
Stop trying to be so rational

Just let
This silly question
Be

54. God is silent
They have no words
Left to speak

55. God is everywhere
God is nowhere

As above
So below

God is right next to me
On the rumbling train

56. God is one mind
Even in a crowded room

57. God is more like a community
For like us all
She cannot survive
As one being alone

58. God is gay
Fuck off

59. God is gay
I'm hurting

60. God is gay
I love you

61. God emits
From a sleepy swamp
Boiling, bubbling
Green, lovely

62. God is
The song of death
That sings for me
Every time I go online and search, "What's causing this headache?"

63. God is the mortar
Between the bricks
Of a public housing complex
That lost its government funding
(But can always get it back)

64. God is the pluck
Of a guitar string
A single vibration
Between the rest

65. God is only a flat pebble
Meant to be skipped across smooth waters

66. God is a bolt of lighting
Striking for a moment
Then gone forever

67. God is red-cherry rose petals
Floating on a glistening river
As a new summer opens its eyes

The delivery truck, on its way to the florist
Slipped on the asphalt
And fell off the bridge
Into the swirling waltz of water below

68. God is the obtuse frills
On paisley curtains
In a room of an old boarding home

Slightly off-putting
But harmless, I guess
I'll try to love it anyway

69. God is a broken bed frame
Leaning tiredly against a
Cracked wall, yellow paint peeling slowly onto the floor

Please, give sympathy to this scene
For though time has dulled its former shine
It carries stories, it carries beauty

Cracks, mold
Bright, cheery

70. God is the glow of a cellphone screen
Twinkling on its charger at night

71. God forgot their password
Again
They tried to click, "forgot password?"
So they could get it emailed to themselves
But alas
God forgot their email password, too

72. God is bees from the hive
Humming through the air
Like little satellites
Orbiting our minds
Like six-legged watches
Ticking away time

73. God is a military satellite system
Blinking stars
Floating across Earth
Watching us, patiently, always

74. God is a long-emptied lake
Dried out by the beating sun
How wonderful
To witness what is left
A great stone hollow
A crater on Earth's skin

75. God lives at the bar
'Cuz he's living in his car
And he buys me a drink
And asks if I can give him
Some place to sleep

76. God is a poorly done comic
You don't get the joke
And quite frankly, you don't want to

77. God is
A paper airplane
Twisting gleefully
Across the classroom
And landing
Just inches
From your desk

78. God is varnished wood
With an amber glow
From the tungsten lights
Hanging overhead

79. God is the string
I cannot cut

80. God is ringing
Like a telephone on the wall
It just keeps ringing, ringing, ringing

81. God is a rock
Stuck to the edge of your chest
And you breathe
And you breathe
And you breathe
And you breathe

82. God is gray
Pulsing
Moving
Breathing
Gray
Like the kid
In my first-grade class
With blue-gray eyes
Gray

83. God is a vision I see
When I close my eyes
There she stands
A vertical line of light
Tearing open
A throbbing split right down my forehead

And every time
She comes to me
I just need
To lie down

84. God is also a serpent
Cast from the garden of Eden
Perhaps the one that tempted Eve
Perhaps not

85. God is a girl
With brown eyes
Pale skin
And teeth
That know how to bite

86. God is a mouth
Tied together with string
Nothing boasts
Yet everything bleeds

87. God is the world I hold onto
Every day, revolving between my steady arms

She spins like the swirl of a stream
The looking-glass river

Sometimes, with every atom of my strength
I try to let her go

But years of her soft humdrum
Have atrophied my forearms to stone

So, wearily, she carries on
And wearily, I watch from above

88. God is not an angry white man in the sky
Or maybe he is, I don't know
But I'm tired of being told that's the only option we have

89. God is hungry
For the hunt

90. God holds our hope
Like a child with a pillowcase full of candy
Fresh from Halloween
An electrified spirit
Bounding up the stairs
With a haul to rival a dragon's hoard

91. God is lines
Of highway light
That stretch, like the wings of a bird
For miles
And miles
And miles
And miles

92. God is blond hair
Blue eyes
Blistered feet
And hideous earrings

93. God is a woman I once saw
Waiting at Chicago O'Hare Airport

I remember her to this day
She wore a purple windbreaker
Gray jeans
And a high ponytail

Cold, unbothered
Seeing her was the moment I knew
Even as life became broken glass
At least I was finally home

94. God is not here
In this room
With me

But I am here
With a dusty fan
Slowly buzzing overhead

95. God is
The tranquility
Of the midwestern United States

These plains
Are one of the few places
My soul feels free to wander

An offering
Of endless sky
Above endless fields

96. God is a worm
That lives inside an apple
A fun surprise (and friend!)
In an already tasty treat

97. God is a sponge
Saturated in soapy sink water
Stuffed beyond satisfaction
Still waiting skeptically
For a squeeze to spill its soak
Onto the stains of Sunday's supper soup

98. God tosses in her sheets
Legs covered in hot and heavy hair

Thick enough to be a forest
Into which she can escape

99. God washes over me
A heaving force as bright as day
As dark as night

100. God asks
No, God demands
That I throw them to the wind
That I kick them off the edge
That I finally let them go

101. God is the woman in the water
Donning a white, flowing gown
With lace flowers embroidered into the hem
Azure waves crash around her
As she sinks
Flows, rises with them

102. God is the truth
A gentle thing
That sits
Between the palms of our hands

103. God is a lie
He, she, ze, they
Were never here
How dare you believe
In the absurdity
Of a plan
Of answers already written
You exist
Only for the sake
Of existing

104. God is self-love
Like the sweet smell of cinnamon
They fill the air
With an elegance
That you breathe deep into your lungs

105. God is self-loathing
Dripping like tar
You wretched, vile beast
A stain on creation's face
Deserve nothing more than suffering
For the treacherous sins
That your arms carried
Into this sick world

106. God is two eyes
Brimming with tears
For the fifth time this week
Such sweet catharsis
Such rough defeat

107. God is our humanity
The one thing we truly share
We are all so fucking connected
Whether we like it or not

108. God heats
The frying pan
Just a little too hot
To properly cook zir chicken

109. God is a painting
How long will you love it?
How long will you
stare

Until you get bored?

110. God slips
like toy slime
Between a child's
hands

Just
make sure
the kid doesn't

eat
it

111. God waits
At the bus sto p
Hiding
under
The bus shelter
While a
light
rai
n

fal
l
s
They'r e
fi ne

Theb us
wi l l

arrive

Inab out

Tw ent ymin utes

112. God
Is
The veins
Of a green leaf
Freshly fallen from the
Autumn branch
Still teeming
With just
The
Teeniest
Bit
Of life

113. God is ivy
Cascading

Down
A
Red
Brick

Home
The
Leaves

Just
Barely
Scrape the

Earth

At
The

Bottom

114. God is the boot
Of a lost hiker
Buried underneath the haunt of redwood trees

Our dear traveler
Scheduled their long-awaited trek
When the forest's river
Was just a tad too high for the trail

115. God loves a good ol' fashioned road trip
I mean, come on
Is there anything better than a long drive
Your favorite music playing
And that pause
When you stop by an off-the-main-road gas station for cheap snacks
Then go out into a cool summer morning
And see the timeless sky above?

116. God can't drive
No, really, she can't
She doesn't see the point
She'd rather take the train

117. God is lost
Amongst the library shelves
Silence sits in the air
Like dust floating in the sunlight

118. God is snot
Dribbling
From the nose
Of a sick toddler

The father wipes it off
And throws it into the trash

119. God is a wall
Up against the sea

God is sticks
Piled onto the ground

120. God is stained-glass windows
Intricately lined, painted ruby and gold
The morning light makes its colors swim on the high church walls

But a shadowed day lies below
Pews filled with black and gray
And at the center, a well-varnished casket
That mirrors a sea of mourners
The silence that hangs above
And stained-glass windows
Of ruby and gold

121. God is
A careful conversation
Between two siblings
Seven years later

122. God waits
At the doctor's office
For the fourth time this month
Xe sighs
But accepts
Xyr unfortunate fate

123. God has
Two thumbs
And both
Are pointed
Down

124. God is
Plantain chips
Covered in coconut oil
With a lime-flavored coating
And ridges
To better the taste

125. God is a computer
With forty-two open tabs

126. God is wondering
If it's time to give up

127. God is swallowing your sorrow
So those you love don't have to eat it, too

128. God stares into the eyes of a soldier
With a gun to her head
And tries to think of what to say

129. God broke

The vase
That sat
On the living room table

Shards of porcelain
Cover the tiled floor
And we must forgive
Like they forgave us

⁂

130. God waits
By the cash register
For her spare change
So finally
She can do
Her laundry

131. God watches
The television screen
For any updates
On I-95 traffic

132. God rolls
Their wheelchair
To the table
For lunch

133. God eats
Pineapple sorbet
But wishes
It was mango

134. God hopes
Faer tax returns
Come soon
The check
Always arrives
Much later
Than fae'd like

135. God sips
Zir morning tea
On the most aureate of days

It is a quiet moment
For a young, quiet soul

136. God drifts
Like the soft wind
That makes green summer leaves dance

137. God is intense
Like fire
Like waves in a storm
Like hair, unkempt
Like wrath, unabated

138. God is emptiness
Sweet, sorrowful emptiness
A hole
Where a heart once beat
A desert
Ignored by the rain

For a season too long

139. God is
A broken love story
Between two friends
Who knew grief
Better than they knew joy

⁂

140. God has learned
How to carry our luggage
With arms that hold tight
And a chest that breathes slowly

141. God bites her fingernails off
Because she can't stand it
When they grow too long

142. God paints
Alone in his backyard shed
Because what else is there to do
When she said it's all wrong

⁂

143. God is lips
On the rim of a just-filled water bottle
The precious tension
Before the reward

144. God is
The hinge on a door frame
That closes slowly
So we can sleep soundly

145. God is
Dehydration
Making your throat sore
Making your head throb
But reminding you
That you can feel
That you are alive
And that you need to function

146. God is a fantasy
So loud
It dims the sound
Of everything else

147. God is a brand-new pair of glasses
Sure, someday they will smudge
But it only takes a quick cloth rub
To see clearly again

148. God loves you
Even when you
Can't love yourself

149. God is soft
Like a fresh cotton blanket
But one that's too thick for a hot summer day
And a little thin for a cold winter night

⌓ ⌓

150. God is a melting ice cube
Stuck under the fridge
Soon to become a pool
For the dog to lick up

151. God is the angst of a teenager
Headbanging to death metal
Waiting for Stacy to text zir back

152. God is
Stale fruit
In the back of your fridge

You swear
You'll eat them soon

But
As always
They rot

⌓ ⌓

153. God is a bitter soul
Muttering to zirself
About how zir cane is too long
And zir liver too short

154. God is a sex worker
Sitting on a park bench
Eating an egg sandwich
Texting her next client
And enjoying the spring day's view

155. God is a wrinkled satin dress
Smoothed out
By Grandma's wrinkled hand

156. God is a bouquet of carnations
Strung onto a wire fence
Always there
Never forgotten

157. If you ever do hear the voice of God
She will tell you that she has lived a long life
And after all her deeds
And misdeeds
She now dreams of things
Like a rose-colored sky
Something, just something
Beyond the same boring blue

158. God is empty chairs
Surrounding an opulent feast

God is an opulent feast
Surrounding empty chairs

God is a dear group of friends
Surrounding an empty table

God is an empty table
Surrounding a dear group of friends

159. I served God a sandwich
At a diner out in Philly
A mustard Rueben sandwich
With a side of sliced vegetables
After he finished, he gave me a 15 percent tip for my service

160. God is a grove of olive trees
Surrounding a concrete wall
Steadfast
Deep roots
Still growing

161. God is a fishing net
Cast beyond the sea
Beyond the Earth, dear Venus,
The Milky Way and all her suns
To something beyond the cosmos
And the time that slivers between them

162. God is the compassion
That glows in our chests

163. God is a thing with sharp edges
That cuts you until you bleed

164. God chews you up
And spits you out like gum

---

165. God is a mystic
Flitting through their perch of the woods
Bitter and cloudy nights bother them none
As the heat of the fire dances on their body
As their feet drum this sacred earth
They know the truth in ways
They alone can grasp

166. God is
The cool breath of reality
One day, it'll push you over
With a thud, you'll fall onto your back
Trapped on the ground, you'll be left
Only to gaze at the muffled sky above

167. God is a moment
Evaporating like a raindrop
In the midday sun
I just needed more time
To learn how to say
Goodbye

168. God has a God
And that God's name
Is God

169. God is that friend of yours
Who moved out to Portland
And now works at a used bookstore
Telling you during the video call
About how they're finally going
To start writing music again

170. God is
The hand of grace
Sweeping down from the sky
Through the ceiling
To your phone
Right before you hit send

171. God, a drag queen, prances across the stage
With a flowing beard and silicone breasts
The emcee, with their tits duct-taped back
And long hair greased up into a bun
Ogles this queer crowd
For every dollar they've got

172. God is the grief I feel when I sit in this elegant room
The emptiness of its forced opulence, a fire that refuses to burn

I wonder if ghosts travel through these walls
If any have lain next to me, hoping they could tell me their story

I wish I could save these spirits
Drown this house in water, let it rot
Let the Earth take it back, let the gold-plated mirrors
Become hidden under a bed of moss

173. God is the Milky Way
With luck, on the clearest of nights
We can witness her stars
The darkness between

But to see is not enough
She is greater
Than we could ever comprehend
Yet still a dot of sand
Amongst the rest of everything

174. God is
The neon sign
Flashing above
The shawarma store
Finally, a North Star
For the young and night-torn
2 a.m. travelers

175. God is moss
That is all
Just moss

176. God is
The red number 2
On the gas station sign
That informs seniors
They get a 20 percent discount

177. God is an abandoned pink rowhouse
With faded paint and a pointed roof
As termites creep into her sinking bones
You speak fondly of the rain-soaked memories
Of summer days spent on her front porch
That you carry with you like a basket of fresh rosemary

178. God is suburbia
A trek across a wintered field of prairie grass
The branches of February trees cracking the sky's blue glass
You hear the soothing sounds of the biting wind
Burning your ears red
And highway cars humming behind you
You see distant clouds lit by a lavender dusk
The village water tower
And a row of houses the size of hotels
Lining the horizon

179. God is a graveyard, centuries old
The souls of the forgotten
Striking their claim
Beside a side-street forest preserve

180. God wishes
On a burned-out star
For another cigarette to smoke
And squash onto the asphalt

181. God holds the sorrow
Of xyr sick, sordid husband
As he drops on the floor
Hollow with regret
And begs for redemption
Amongst the splintered wood

182. God is an old attic : -)

183. God is two friends holding hands
A friendship as long
As both of them have lived

184. God looks toward the sky
And does his best
To ignore
The honking cars
Behind him

185. God races on the track
Destined for third place
But she holds out hope
For the someday promise of silver

186. God embraces her weeping son
With a splinter on the side of his pinky toe
She knows that without her love
He'd be just destined to die

187. God
Sick, drunk
Takes a piss
In the dirty pub bathroom
With music pumping
From the dance floor outside

They wonder
How they got so lucky
To be alive
In this very moment

188. Our God is a stubborn God
Like a wool blanket
Whose rough fibers
Can scratch the skin
Rash and scab the skin
But these coarse bristles
Are what keep them together, at least so far

189. God is the anxious writer
Who overflows with brilliance
Yet cannot
Spill anything
Onto paper

190. God is a bruise
From the rubber bullet of a policeman's gun
Puncturing a proud, terrified body and soul
Who believes in the duty
Of fighting for a better world
And is forced to suffer for it

191. God sits
At her computer
Finishing up yet another work project
As twilight twinkles its lilac perfume
She is determined to prove
That she *deserves* to be there, okay?

192. God is an internet troll
With furious fingers that can really type
But never truly win

193. God wishes
Zi hadn't said
What zi just said

Father, Jesus, Holy Spirit, and Son
It would be okay

It would just be okay

If zi'd just learned to shut

Zir foolish mouth

194. God is

The ribs

Of a rat

As they

Dissolve

In the stomach

Of a snake

195. God is
The foam of the sea
That bubbles beside
The foaming mouth
Of a rabid raccoon (which is also God)

196. God is
The accent over the letter "u"
In the word, "tú"

◇ ◇

197. God is a desire for adventure
Larger than life
Constantly craved
Until every corner of the world
Has been swallowed like soup

198. God is the speck of uncertainty
That makes life all the more exciting
And all the more awful

199. God wants
Nothing more
Than a happy wife
Happy kids
And a loving neighborhood

200. God has roots
That crawl as deep
As the bedrock itself

◇ ◇

201. God is a color palette
Of yellow
Against orange
Against beige
Against blue

202. God is sage green
Next to a tawny brown
And a candy-apple red

203. God is a C-sharp key
Stuck down

On a decrepit piano

From the player who played

Years and years ago

But didn't feel like fixing what broke

Stuck as it is

God is in constant action

Yet completely silent

204. God is a pair of hands
Scorched red and raw
From the friction of climbing rope
Grasping for just a little too long
But still trying to climb

205. God is
The piece of tape
You put over
Your laptop camera

206. God is the bitter taste of motherwort
My favorite nighttime tea, paired with lemon balm
She comforts me, holds me close so I feel safe
But I wish she could make me fall asleep
Not just lay in bed for a three-hour, half-awake haze

I'm working to trust love again, I really am
But I'm so, so very tired

207. God knows nothing
Sees nothing
Feels nothing
Says nothing
Is nothing

208. God is the lamp above the drawing board
Illuminating a new sketch
Soon to be processed and ready for the market

The artist's cigarette burns between their fingers
Ash from the old ones squished
Onto the corner of their desk, remaining uncleaned

209. God is the bead store
Between Willard Street
And Barrymore Avenue
Eighteen years
A tiny profit
A quiet town

210. God is bad takeout
From that place you always order from
Today, you got just a touch of food poisoning

But
Let's be real
You love their food, it's cheap
You'll probably order from them again

211. God is
The rolling country road
That you dream of driving down
But would hate to live by
Too many crickets, too many crickets, all summer long

212. God is strategic
Fae plays the system
Like a blackjack dealer at the casino

What would happen
If we broke the rules?

213. God is healing, yes
But more like a lotion
Not meant for your sensitive skin

She will soften you, yes
Fills all the cracked creases
Burning onto your forehead
But be warned, she'll make prancing
Pricks of red dance out of your pores, too

214. God, as lines of binary code
Wonders what would happen
If they added the number "two"

⚭ ⚭

215. God is trapped
Caged at a train station
City buildings, like angels
Surround the stars dotting the night sky

What a wondrous sight to behold
Yet xe cannot cast xer gaze above xer feet
Standing at the center of the sweet, cement platform

216. God flings his arms
Toward the temple
Of the forgotten
A thick marble slab
Cut to reflect
The heartache of Father
Who lost Son
Between fine grains of sand

⚭ ⚭

217. God orbits above the atmosphere
You try to speak to them
As their satellite mind
Crosses your night

218. God's toothy smile
Lights up the family dinner table
A bright excitement
Behind the potato salad

219. God is
The list of friends
You keep in your journal
To remind yourself
That you are loved
So deeply
So very, very deeply

220. God is a list
Of recently used emojis
On your battered cellphone
The classic side-eyes
Next to a peach
Next to a sun

221. God is
Beautiful bullshit
With just a bit
Of lavender-infused honey

222. God slips through my fingers
Like sand
Like dust
Like water
Like smoke

223. God is a postmodernist
For him, it's all a social construct
A self-imposed myth in our mind
Yet still we live its lessons on the daily

224. God is materialistic
Don't get me wrong
They love you, they want to help you
But at the same time
That can get in the way of their other handsome Love
Their brand new, flat-screen TV
It has all these great shows
That silence their soured mind for a bit

225. God loves her cherished wife
Who always makes the best breakfast
Fried eggs
A side of bacon
And a small bowl of cherry yogurt

226. God loves
Her only daughter
Sent to our Earth
To touch our blistered hands
And guide us toward something beyond
The apparition of what we were told was true freedom

227. God loves her singing mother
Who birthed her from the sky
And bathed her in river water

Today, as her mother retires to the fire
God rests on the cool Earth
Looking toward the stars

228. God loves her stuck-up sister
Her nose always tipped
Just a little too high
Yet she never quite fell over

◇ ◇

229. God is
A Swedish baker
In a pink, printed skirt
And a dusty brown smock

230. God is a Black woman
Who likes to sing in the shower
In the spring, she gets lost in the azaleas
That bloom through the holes of her fence every year

She's trying to break up with her boyfriend but hates confrontation
So is struggling to set up that last date

She loves her job, hates her commute
And swears there's a ghost living in the basement
But, she hopes, a friendly one

231. God is
The vitamin D
Circulating the veins
Of a mid-Atlantic salmon

232. God is
The delightful fluoride
Pumped into your drinking water

233. God is cold coffee
In a Styrofoam cup
The man running between work meetings
Keeps forgetting to drink it
But he'll get to it
Eventually, in time, maybe

234. God has a heart of gold
Lungs filled with bronze
And kneecaps made of steel

235. God's a successful entrepreneur
Whose world-renowned athletic enterprise
Produces millions (perhaps billions!) of shoes every year

Rumbling underneath his feet
The floor-level factory workers
Churn their days away
So his empire can burst with sole-filled glory

As far away, faceless laborers
Sweat in globalized fields
So these shoes can breathe out polyester miracles

Benedictions bathing the feet of their buyers
Worthy of his fortune's hard-earned rewards
The life he built around it

Yet at the end of the day
When the warehouse doors close
And the sun sets half a world away

When the weary workers trudge home
To rest beside the ones they love
Is God's world still running?

236. God is the moringa leaf
That clears the mind
And nourishes the body

237. God is the eucalyptus leaf
That I put in my bath
Because I read in a book
It can wash away grief
And clear out my sinuses
It definitely helped
But it also clogged the drain

238. God is the feminine and the masculine
Holding hands, rolling down a river side by side

239. God still hasn't done
The fucking dishes

240. God is
A boulder
That fell
Off the North Rim
Of the Grand Canyon

Two tourists
Driving all the way
From Tulsa, Oklahoma

Caught the awesome sight
Just moments
Before

The crash
At the bottom

241. God is eons
And eons
And eons
And eons

242. God stretches
Far and wide
Throughout the cosmos
Beyond the limits of the universe
Perceived and hidden from our view

Yet at the same time
God stretches throughout the
Smallest, most precious spaces
A web between the gaps of our fingers

What a blessing
To be big, to be small
Everything, and nothing
All at once

243. God is writing
For the sake of writing
For the sake of writing
For the sake of writing

244. God is the grime
Stuck between your fingernails

245. God speaks to you
Not as an earth-shattering voice
Booming from the clouds

But as a one-footed pigeon
Hobbling toward you at the park
Cooing for some of your sandwich breadcrumbs

246. God is a single spider, spinning her web
A home made of silk
Held together by oak branches
She watches her forest intently

247. God is poorly made
Like a knitted blanket
Whose creator stitched with such rich love
But the hands of a beginner

248. God is
The practice
Of cleaning as you go

Picking up a discarded sock
On the way to your room

Taking dirty dishes to the kitchen
Before you cook dinner

Little reminders
Throughout the day
That you, too
Can keep the world from chaos

249. God is
A broken glass bottle
Shattered by a drunk man on the road
Zi wishes
Zi had more time
To exist as a whole

250. God's words
Are meaningless
Don't listen to a single one
Throw out your Bible
Run from the cathedral

The wisdom of the ones you love
And even those you hate
Screams the truth more loudly
Than any gospel could dare try

251. These words
Of God
Are mine
And mine alone

Stop!

Please

Stay over there
And let me carry

These precious hymns
In solitude

252. God is ridiculous
Who came up with this crap?
You know better than to believe such nonsense

253. God is a three-letter word
We throw around
For salvation
Bow until your back aches
Pray until your hands bleed
Submit to this word:

God

G O D

Whatever he is
Just believe in him
And I swear
Everything will be okay

254. God is sinking

Sinking

Sinking

Sinking

Can you feel her heartbeat from afar?

255. God is

O

G

D i

S

G

O

D

i

S

F

O

R

G

O

T

T

E

N

256. God washes down
A bus-station sink

257. God is
A crooked spine
Curling slowly
Into a sturdy knot

258. God is broad daylight
That's just
A little too hot
A little too blue
But surely none of that
Is important to you

259. God scrolls
Her red, neon words
Across the subway train arrival tracker

A single commuter
Lifts his heavy eyes
To read a bitter commandment
Of a thirty-three-minute wait

260. God is lost thoughts
Scattered, brushed away
Like red paint
On a white canvas

261. God is an intern
Dressed in the tailored slacks
His mother bought him last week
And the slick leather sneakers
His grandfather used to wear

Finely tuned hair
A smile to rival a magazine cover's shine
This man
Is in the perfect condition
To be spat on
Through the front-desk phone receiver

262. God clenches shiny coins
She stole from another man's bag
In her soft, stinky arms

She wonders what would happen
If she bit into them

263. God is unemployed
And still living in a hostel
With a shitty Wi-Fi connection

She sits on the shore
Of South Beach, Miami Beach
Hefty clouds above
The setting sun poking out of the sea

Crystal-clear water in front
Vibrant pastel buildings
And pumping clubs behind

Everything is just fine

264. God is
Shoe scruffs
On the schoolhouse wall
A small mess
Flush with a winding mansion of memories

265. God is
The series of choices
That brought you
To where you are
Today

266. God swims around
The pink teapot
Fae love to call home
Like a fish
Fae leap
Scurry
And dive

267. God is small
So very, very small
Atoms are like galaxies
Quarks the stars

A part of the whole, a snippet

But when they move
The world moves with them

268. God is a full moon
Floating up
Like a silver bubble in the sky
A glowing stone
Ready to pop
And set the tides
Into disarray

269. God is a woman
Sleeping on the ground
Asleep for so long
We fear she'll never wake up

But come
If you look closely
You will see the birth of wily dandelions
Growing on her side

270. God is
A chipped tooth
From a nice punch
To a mean face

271. God is a proud mountain
Viewed on an online map
By a teenager
In Ulaanbaatar, Mongolia

272. God is the needles
Pricking the back
Of a first-time acupuncture patient
I hope you can get some relief, dear friend

273. God is
A single grain of corn
Consumed
By a gleeful grasshopper

274. God sometimes likes
To sit on the floor
To do something
A little different
Than stand on his feet

275. God is the two minutes
Before your lunch break

276. God is an old game show
Viewed on daytime television
And absolutely nothing else

277. God
Wants to swallow
The television set

278. God has 186 teeth
And is immensely proud
Of every single one

279. God's just a weird little guy to be honest

280. God is your favorite poetry teacher
Hunched forward at his desk
The wheels of his chair would squeak
As he turned to the neat rows of desk before him
With a spark in his eye
And mole on his lower lip

He told stories of the writer
That lives in every pen
Every untied shoe
Every half-asleep dreamer

281. God is
Just being kind to yourself
Forgiving your past mistakes
Lacing your arms around your chest
And heaving a sigh of relief

282. God is searching for words
That they can never seem to find
But they're hoping that somehow
Through sin or through glory
Their message still reaches us

283. God is something we put up with
Like the full-mouthed snores of a loved one
Because, despite the headaches
And many hours we spend awake
Wondering why we were cursed to deal with this
The warm embrace they bring to our life
Reminds us that living without them
Would probably be fine, but something would always be missing

284. God is
The yellow stripe
On the rainbow flag
The energy
That powers
A revolution

285. God is a triangle
A circle
A square
And a pentagon
All superimposed
On top of each other

Photo description: a pencil drawing done by me that visually demonstrates the last poem—a triangle, circle, square, and pentagon superimposed on top of each other. To the right is an arrow pointing toward this shape labeled "God."

286. God is just all vibes, man

⚇ ⚇

287. God is the feeling of indecision
Frozen like an iceberg
Melting, the sun cakes beads of sweat onto its skin

Eventually, the once-frigid beast will crack in half
Its weight crashing atop you
Shoving you into the ocean's death

So, before it does, you have to jump
With faith and freedom as all you carry
Because then, as hard as it is
You can finally swim yourself to safety

288. God swims
Across the Atlantic Ocean
She claims she takes this journey
To redeem us from our sins
But almost no one is watching
And those that do
Don't understand the meaning

289. God
Like Icarus
Flew just a little too high
But let us remind him
That underneath his melted wings
He has the sea to catch him

290. God is a child
Resting on her couch after school
The living room may be a boring, trinket-filled trudge
The couch a stoic friend, indeed

But when she closes her eyes
The room fades into a baby-blue sky
Encircling an endless ocean
The couch a small boat flowing atop the waves

What a perfect image
For God is a creature of imagination
Who quietly lives in a lucid dream

291. God is a plunger
On the side
Of a gas station bathroom
He has the job
That absolutely no one wants
But understands
It is the job he is meant to do

292. God is an online tarot card reader
A form of modern-day oracle

In the course of an hour
They'll shine a light into your spirit
Blow away the dust filling your mind's cabinets

Through the bond of the digital landscape
You will learn to understand
That the truth is not yet written, but instead
Fate and free will are lovers that like to gossip
Of what may come your way
What may hold you back
What may carry you forward

293. God is
Two moths
Flying around
An abandoned church
And landing on the same window

294. God holds out his arm
To keep the train doors open
For a frantic commuter sprinting across the platform

He doesn't know
If his arm will be chopped in two
From the jaws of this brash metal beast

But, determined
His arm remains stiff
Understanding what it feels like
To dash with such vigor
And still lose the race

295. God dreams
Of everlasting life
But knows
That with three kids to raise
In this two-bedroom home
Such an idea
Would cost more
Than she could ever afford

296. God is Black, God is Brown
God's divine right is to walk down the street
As the truth whose only myth
Is the risk of them ever facing harm

297. God is an Arab woman
Who screams at the sight of suffering
Whose honeycomb words
Will never be yours to hold
If you can't carry her, too

⌁ ⌁

298. If God is all things
God must be Lucifer, too

299. If God is all things
God must be everyone, everything that's ever hurt us
Beat us, manipulated us
Was proud to bear the duty
Of drilling our souls
With the bitter belief that we are nothing more than dust

When should we forgive? Understand that they are hurting, too?
When is it better to link arms with our sacred rage?
What answers I carry with these words
What reflections God has for this little poem, too
I simply cannot say

300. God is a situationship
Oh shit! Oh fuck!
Get out, get out now! You want nothing to do with that.

⌁ ⌁

301. God is a $20 donation
To a mutual aid fundraiser
For your friend's top surgery

302. God is the redness in your eyes
        When you cry
        When you smoke
        When you protest
        In the streets

303. God reminds you
    That it has to get done
    That it doesn't matter
    How it gets done
    With sweat, blood, teeth ground down
    With knives cutting through your bones
    Or saltwater flooding your lungs

    It just really
    Really needs
    To get done

304. God is an aphid
    That landed on a rose stem
    A little lime dot
    Crawling
    All about
    They are
    Too small
    To feel
    The thorn's nasty prick

305. God is for sale
On a new plot of land
Where the mango tree
Used to stand

306. God is
The lyrics
At the height
Of Perfume Genius's song, "Queen"

No family is safe
While I sashay

307. God is
Blinking headlights
On the other side of
The parking lot

308. God is a lounge of lizards
Contrasting the bleached summer sidewalk
As a stark, saturated green

309. God is your septum
Swollen from the pinch
Of a brand-new, silver-steel piercing
(So, if you can, try not to sneeze for a bit cuz it'll be
really hard to wipe out the snot. Trust
me, I know.)

310. God fishes on a silver pond
Colored by a shining light
Beaming up from the surface
While above, graying clouds
Weigh down the sky

311. God is a prairie blazing star
Wild grass rising high in an otherwise low-grown field
While her leaves dream of kissing the sun
Long, winding roots leave her half underground
So, instead, she compromises
And sways with the sound
Of chirping crickets in the night

312. God is a meadow of goldenrod
Yellow flowers bursting open, blooming right as fall
Begins to cast its gaze toward the ground

Green leaves of sugar maple fade into orange
The sky grays, the trees become bare
As night blinks its eyes open for winter

This remains the lesson of time's ever-spinning wheel
Sometimes, something within us has to die
For the gardens of spring to be born into our lives

So, keep your heart open, too
For the goldenrod signs of when that time
Of a beautiful death is coming

313. God is an arrow
Pointed upward
On a bow
With its string stretched thin

The precious tension
Before the release

314. God is a flavor
Beyond what our tongues can taste
But sometimes, we can smell it
Underneath our sticky shoes

315. God is a shadow
Trailing you down the alley
On a moonlit night

316. God floats
To the surface
As you sink
Into the riverbed

317. God plunges down the sinkhole
As you climb to the mountain's peak

318. God falls from the sky
Like the soft rain of a heaving storm

319. God is the Tower of Babel
Struck down by his own pounding rage

It's true, they say
That nothing lasts forever
Yet here you are
Broken bricks and all

320. God is
A rotting woodside cabin
Filled with a hollow silence
Dust with a death wish
A spider spinning soliloquies into her web

Hushed, it waits
For the swift return of summer
A sun to warm its sweet decay

⁂

321. God is a forest filled with birch trees
Stand before it
And each tree is their own soul
Separately together like the lines of a barcode

But bike along the trail
And suddenly, they blur
Into a single, white canvas
For your mind to fill as you rush down the road
The endless, soothing road

322. God is the smile of your lover
An ecstasy between their teeth
That shines brighter
Than any star would ever dare

323. God is serendipity
These two things
Were always meant to meet

⁂

324. God
Is like
When you wash your hands
Without soap
Enough
To make you *feel*
Like you at least *tried*
But not enough
To get the job done

325. God is
Stubby fingers
On a cello
Two sizes
Too big

This isn't
Your fault
I promise

326. God is an online forum
Where people post photos they took or found
That, through timing
And through luck
End up looking like a Renaissance masterpiece

Beauty doesn't exist
Only where we're told
It's supposed to be

327. What would it be like
To go on a date with God?
This is another poem
Where I'd prefer to ask
As opposed to try and answering
Though I'd love to hear your thoughts

328. God is a door
Ripped out of its frame
Come see me on the other side
I swear I'm always here

329. God is when, instead of a door
You have strings of beads in the doorframe

Green, brown, shining
Not a solid barrier
But an invitation—with boundaries

330. God is the elegance of the perfect arch
Made when a car backs slowly
Into a thin parking space

331. I don't know if God understands emotions
'Cuz like, how can a light
An energy
A physical sensation
That drives down the back of your neck

How can something that isn't living
That is barely a thought, an awareness
Even begin to explore our blood that courses
With the strange ethers of joy, sorrow
Hopelessness, love?

332. God slips
On a floor
Just recently cleaned

If only
The "Wet Floor" sign
Was snapped out
Onto the tiles

333. God's an inhaler
For a kid diagnosed with asthma
But unfortunately, diagnosed in what is today called the United States

Faer dad had to be on the phone for three hours
When insurance said they'd cover it
But the pharmacist at the counter said they had to pay full price
And the pharmacist's boss isn't sure what to do, did they enter the bin number right?
And the lady at the doctor's front desk said there might be a copay, but it shouldn't
be over $35
Because they hit their deductible last month
But that's still a lot of money for Dad
And the call to the insurance company kept dropping because of bad data coverage
And the robotic phone menu is impossible to navigate
And it's just

334. God swims through my open eyes
Like a fish out of water
Like a sun without her moon

335. God is redeemed
When she returns to the water

Sink, float
Live, die
Breathe, rest

336. God is a flaky friend
Who tells you how they'll always be there
Through the thick and the thin
The oil and the water

Yet here you stand
Alone on a roadside corner
The sky wearing a weary gray

And honestly, you feel like falling
Nose to the ground
Bleeding through your teeth

You really needed a friend today
But they just break you

God, I really needed a friend today
But you just break me

337. God is a transaction
You give them your prayers
They give you what you want
Or what you need
Or whatever is best for you
Maybe even something bad
If you don't ask the right way
It's not quite clear what you're getting back

338. God is radioactive waste
Come too near
And she'll creep into you
Like a cancer, a weapon
A wretched wave of destruction

But don't scorn her
Throw stones at her running muck
Because it's not her fault
She can't help how she exists

339. God is the effect of the cause
And the cause of the effect

But enough about me
How about you?
How are you today?

⚭ ⚭

340. God is huddled over a table
In a quiet coffee shop
Hands clasp a white mug
Filled with zir favorite oolong tea

A moment beyond time, thriving
Zir lipstick stains the rim of the cup

341. God is the confusion
When you are told
To honor a mother
And a father

But you look up
And instead see two mothers
Who poured like honey
Into your heart

342. God is the children
Who took the wrong path
When they wandered through the woods
Rich with despair
He will never find the light
She will never be forgiven

As age bakes on
To their rumpling skin
When their bones start to break, they will collapse onto the road

On their backs, their eyes will catch a glimpse
Of a bright sky between jagged branches

They will recognize
They were right
To never turn back

343. God sweats tears of joy
At the midsummer baseball game
As her son glides his leg into a homerun

The aluminum bench sizzles her skin
A poorly cooked burger churns in her stomach
But none of that matters
As pride sweeps across
Her sunburnt, mosquito-bitten face

344. God is all of us trying to reconfigure what life means in the age of COVID-19

A global fucking pandemic
I can barely type this poem out

About half of these poems were first written just months before it happened
Before something catastrophic
Something painfully universal pushed us to the ground

Into lives stretched thin from online funerals, triaged hospitals
Pharmaceutical companies denying half the world vaccines
Willing to let countless people die so they could make a profit

The weight of not knowing when or if it will ever end
Even as mountains kept still, the wind kept blowing
Birds flew and flowers bloomed

...

This poem came three years later
When our sideways world was still rocking, just differently
When sick lungs still collapsed, the news just wasn't covering it

What happens to the spirit when so deeply challenged?
When every breath you take is a minefield
When as a community loneliness is soaked into our bones
When we learn to love with such depth
That we put on a mask
Because we care for our neighbors?

What happens to my words, our words
When every ounce of ourselves is rearranged?

Sometimes, I write these poems to understand God
Sometimes because I don't even know what needs to be asked

345. God is the entanglement of everything in this earth
Like mycelium roots, connecting trees, cicadas, bacteria
The yeast flowering in our guts

We can choose to believe we are on top
Of a hierarchy that heaven built
But instead, we must embrace the blessing
That the world is too complex
For one hero amongst the rest
We are a knotted game of cat's cradle
A beautiful cycle, a death
A heartbreak, a grieving, a miracle

346. God is The Day After
The Day After the last US bomb is dropped
Over Somalia, Yemen
Over Palestine by Israel's war planes

The Day After US sanctions are lifted
In Zimbabwe, Iran, North Korea, Cuba

The Day After every cowardly political intervention
By the CIA ends abroad and in the United States

After Hawaiians no longer are forced to live with water
Tainted by US military bases

I could try to depoliticize
To recognize God in the shrapnel that left children's corpses crushed
And burned from bombs that never should have been dropped

In the backs turned
From Palestinians having their homes bulldozed by Israel's military
Or starving Yemenis brutalized by Saudi Arabia's blockade

Expand God toward a debate, a robotic exercise of thought
But simply, I cannot, I will not

God is only The Day After
These man-made horrors end
And liberation
Is but a small swim away

347. God melts
Like ice cream into a new linen couch
Quite a sticky mess
To find stuck to your thighs

348. God is the popping noise
Made when you crack neck

A sign of a released relief for your spine
A bloody nuisance for your neighbor's ears

349. God needs to be watered
Like a plant, to grow
But pour too much
And she will wither
The same as if
She were left dry

350. God carries dirt in his palms
It spills from the crack
Between his two hands

351. God is a metaphor

Perhaps for something valiant and holy
Perhaps for something wretched that flies with feathered wings
Perhaps for the residue of something lost
To time that we wish we could cling to

The meaning is not too obvious
But at least we're trying to make sense of it

352. God is a myth we sing to ourselves
To help us sleep on melancholy nights

353. God is a back
Curled up on a grimy bed

Sometimes, when life feels a size too big
We shrink ourselves, swallowing shame like it's our medicine
But now, at the witching hour

We can shape ourselves into a seed
And let our roots grow fat as trees
Until the someday sprouted leaves
Are finally home against the breeze

354. God is alive!
A being, wet
Throbbing, walks among us!

The gift of knowing sweat and vomit
They are our flesh and equal

The curse of knowing that this means
They soon must die, too

355. God is a lightswitch
Turned off for the night
Heavy, he hangs down

356. God is a carrot
That you munch munch munch munch munch

It cracks like a finger
And is swallowed like a dagger

357. God is envious
Of our awesome sky
For it only has to exist
Before our sacred hearts
To be understood
As holy

358. God is the trauma
We carry in our bones
Where in this life
Does suffering have meaning?

359. God is silence
Shaken, sacred
Savory silence

360. God is a hospice
There is little hope for life
Between these thin walls
But still there remains comfort in knowing
We had time to say goodbye

361. To say that God could never be the darkness
Forgets the many blessings
Found in the absence of light

On the most unbearable summer days
Where would you rather be?

Under the direct heat of the sun
Or in the shade?

How boring would our world be
If it lacked the depth gifted to us by shadows?
And everything was all just a constant, stoic
Bulging, burning brightness?

If we never were able to close our eyes
Get away from the frantic hues of life
Forget about it all and dream?

362. God is an online ad
For a foam cylinder
You roll on your back
To crack out the kinks

363. God is
A hot chili pepper

You pop it into your mouth
And feel your gums ignite

364. God is a fart
And as such
Reminds us
Of the most important commandment
That he who hath smelt it
Must indeed have dealt it

◇ ◇

365. God sets her daily alarm for 6 a.m.
Though time, for her, is meaningless
It's nice to wake up early enough for breakfast

366. God is the map
Of glow-in-the-dark stars
Stuck to the ceiling of a child's bedroom

They teach us that even the smallest of spaces
Can become a universe

367. God is my grandma's mouse-shaped telephone
Standing up, the yellow receiver curled up against his plastic ear
As a child, seeing it felt like …
Honestly, it's beyond words

Less a feeling, more a place
A dusty basement, donut shaped
Cement-floored, with creaky stairs down the middle

His former home
One of many dolls, wind-up toys
Sheets and knotted yarn

All stacked and squished in
Boxes, tables
Cabinets, on top of old rocking chairs
He was beloved in a sea of antique community

But now, he sits alone
Next to my father's work desk
A statue of something and someone loved
Marking the memories of what's now gone

368. God's eyebrow is pierced
The left one, to be specific
The skin, unfortunately
Is slightly infected

369. God is the horizon
The thin line
That divides the finite Earth
From the infinite sky

370. God is
Experimental jazz
Chaos
But there's a rhythm to it

371. God is a magnificent stretch
To the inner thigh

372. God is
The joy and relief
Of finally finding
An open wall socket

373. God is the stories
We share in community
The mortar that keeps us
Together as spirits

Because without it
Every word that flows from the pen
Or is sprinkled by the rain

Will still fade from the page
Or be dried out by the sun

And we are not meant to disappear

374. God is waiting for her next hit
The adrenaline surge, the rapture she needs
When her life feels like a ghost

I hope she knows
That even in her loneliness, we are with her
As she sweats through the sheets
We love her, always

375. God forgives
But honestly, sometimes we don't
And that's fine
We can find other ways to move on

376. God squeezes your sins
Between her meaty legs
Until, from the pressure, they pop

Observe, as shining pus flows
From the center of the tear

377. God is a theater cast made up of a thousand actors
In front of an audience of one

378. God is the wondrous viola instrument
Curved into an orchestra with all the rest

Our dear viola
Is usually forgotten from the musical mix
Some of us may not even know their name
Yet, without them, the music is incomplete

379. God is a bass drum
Whose beat rings loud
Through the towering walls
Of the great symphony hall

380. God is a trail of fluorescent lights
Lining a parking lot at night
Like looming saints
Holding up a heavy sky

381. God is
A story
That erupts
From our throat
Like a song
Like a bird
Dying to be free

382. God is a comfortable chair
One of those fancy ones
Always on display at US department stores
With all those gadgets, like cupholders, phone charging ports
Even a built-in back massager

While shopping for a new doormat
A passing couple can't help but stare
Curious if such a circus of a sofa
Would ever fit in their milk-crate-sized apartment

383. God is the modern hustle
Pushing through the muck
The gelatin
The potpourri pudding

384. God is
An opportunity
You almost missed

385. God is the roof of a gas station
Just enough shelter
From the pouring rain
For customers to fill up their tank

⚭ ⚭

386. God writes
Xyr sacred poetry
With a pencil in xyr mouth
And a wad of gum in xyr hair

387. God is staring out a window
At a lofty palm tree
As it sways in the wind
Of an approaching hurricane

388. While roaming through the neighborhood
God hears a crunch beneath their shoe
And looks down to see a golden necklace
With a tear-shaped pendant
Holding a pearl at its center

Left on the sidewalk
By a woman who has yet to notice
It's gone

389. God is a purse hook
Under the table
Of a local dive bar

390. God is
A game of checkers
At a quiet midtown park

391. God is
Hot sauce
Dribbled over
Your fresh
Chocolate
Croissant

392. God is mild heartburn
Enough to be a nuisance
But not enough to make you worry

393. God is a teenager's first ear piercing
Poked into their earlobe on their thirteenth birthday
At the kiosk shop just outside the food court
Their friends surrounding them, grinning widely
At the rebellious stud of cubic zirconia

394. God is a cheap necklace
Sterling silver in the shape of a Celtic knot

I bought it at a tourist shop in Galway
A quick stop before hopping on the bus back to Dublin

Worn around my neck for almost a year
I felt like I could tell stories
Of a long-ago home that I almost understood
That I maybe understood
That I want to understand

395. God is the prick
Of a tattoo needle
Curving onto a woman's hip
Self-discovery in the form
Of a pastel-brown bunny

396. God is a fat woman
Thick curves where her hips meet her waist
Form tall, sloping mountains for the sun to shine through

Stretch marks become cascading rivers feeding the plains
Keeping the fields alive, the bees buzzing
Twisting honey for your ravenous tongue

The drooping skin below her upper arms
What miraculous cliffs!
Tourists travel for days just to catch a glimpse

Her body is rich with life
Teeming with forests, deserts, swamps, dunes
A haven for us to offer our softest love

397. God is my grandfather's hands
Veins popping out
Red blood appears blue underneath his skin
I look to my own veins trailing my wrist
And see that I bleed blue, too

398. God is a lily pad
Atop the ripples of the pond
She blooms freely
And smiles deeply
Where her leaves part

399. God dreams
Of silk
Of rubber
Of manicured nails

400. God is nauseous
Sick in bed for over a week
Sick in bed for the eighth time this year

Yet even in these hushed moments
They are holy

401. God is only human
And to expect anything more
Is pretty much pointless

402. God is truth
Though a truth
That allows for
An occasional white lie

403. God is for the patient
God is for the kind
And God is for the beautiful
The ones you'd never leave behind

404. God is a cup overflowing
With raspberry lemonade
That gurgled from the soda machine
Just a little too quickly

405. God is the greasy letter "J"
On a laptop keyboard

406. God is
The ridges of a key
Being ripped across
The edge of a wooden table
What an irritating sound
What an inane way to destroy furniture

407. God will never be Manifest Destiny
The great woman who treks the land
Leaves footprints like craters on a desolate moon

408. God is so close
To divine perfection

But zi has this one piece of lettuce stuck in zir teeth that zi can't quite seem to get out

409. God is the static before a storm
Like a radio wave swimming through the air
What message did she write onto your prickled skin?

410. God scratches off
Another lottery ticket
A pile of losers
Stacked on the floor

411. God is a paper crown
Placed on the head
Of a fussy child
For her third birthday

412. God rides
In the back of a limousine
With the tinted windows up
For though he adores his fans
He needs his personal space, too

413. God decided to copyright his Holy Bible
For after so much sale and global distribution
It only seems fair he receives compensation
For his consecrated words

414. God is
The ritual sacrifice
Of a dead houseplant
To the temple
Of the trash can

415. God is an essence
That taste like sea salt
And reeks of skunk

416. God is but
A trick of the mind
That wink of pareidolia
Boasting an illusion we create in the mirror
So it's not our own face we have to see looking back

417. God is a bowl
Packed with fresh indica
Hope you can enjoy your high, my friends

418. God doesn't care
If you've sinned
Or if you've saved

Only if you test the bathwater
Before you bathe

419. God is the fire alarm
Whose batteries you keep forgetting to change

Beep

Beep

Beep

Beep

Beep

420. God lives
Inside a teardrop

As sorrow
Falls from your eye
She guides her way
Down your jaw

And drips
Ever so quickly
To the ground
To remind you

That she'll always be
Right beneath your feet

421. God is a mosaic
Of round pebbles
Redeemed thumbtacks
And cherished glasses frames

It drops onto the ground
And shatters into a million pieces
In this act, it becomes
An even more profound piece of art

422. God gives our worries to the waves
For though she can carry them
The sea understands sorrow
Better than she ever could

423. God is the scream
That lives in your chest

God is the scream
That lives in your chest

God is the scream
That lives in your chest

God is the scream
That lives in your chest

God is the scream
That lives in your chest

424. God is a compass
That points to the east
Toward where the sun rises
And the new day begins

425. God is bored
Of the heavens and the Earth
How dull it is, every day
Bearing witness to the same light of the same sky
The same water that divides the same lands

Something, oh something
Must be ripening just beyond this

426. God's favorite thing
Is the plastic bag full of batteries
They keep in a drawer under the kitchen counter

427. God bleeds between my teeth
And throbs within my gums
She lives as my sore reminder
That I really need to floss more

428. God is Mexican, Belarusian
Finnish, Nigerian
Japanese, Samoan
Iranian, Moroccan
Indonesian, and hates how ice tastes when it's crushed

429. God lives
In Santa Fe
At faer age, who wouldn't?
Relatively cheap living options
Perfect weather
And gorgeous, natural scenery

430. God is in-between
But never in the middle

431. God created our world
Through their spit
Through their vomit
Through their tears
Through their snot

432. God trails her voice
Until it becomes
A path, a sidewalk, a road
A network
Of interstate highways
Criss-crossing into a soup bowl
That she eats from with a spoon
Down the same mouth
Where it all began

433. God wins
Every game
Of poker
He doesn't cheat
He doesn't lie
He's really just that good

434. We say everything holds beauty
Like water spilling from your cup

But God is quite an ugly thing
No arch licked with gold nor wild prairie field

Colors clash, sewage reeks from their skin
And when we see it, our eyes bulge
Nostrils flare

We turn our cheek from them while claiming we kissed
it

Why do we need God to be beautiful?
What of the haggard you cannot pour from your cup?
Do we not worship them, too?

435. God's our omnipotent scapegoat
God is all the terrified gay girls
God's an artificial construct
God's your favorite guy at the potluck

436. God just wants
To make you feel bad
Because, you too
Have hurt them
In more ways
Than they could ever count

437. God is when a building is actually designed for
wheelchair-users

438. God bears no special talents
No magic skills
But they can type a decent email
Without typos
Without dangling modifiers
Without flowery sentences
That distract the reader from the main point

439. God is transgender
For the same way some say on each of the seven days
Creation bloomed something new
So, too, do we
And so, too, does God
Become more than what we were told
Is only one possible stagnant truth
And push us to do the same

440. God sits
On zir rocking chair
In a sunflower-patterned dress
On a wooden front porch
On a hot summer night

It's zir favorite place
To keep for zirself

⟜ ⟜

441. With time, your soul will be lost
Dissolved from every heart's memory
You will only live on
As a grain-of-salt picture
That God stores on their laptop

442. God is writing a book
That contains the narrative
Of all of our lives
Detailing every human, every bird
Every blade of prairie grass
Every rock, every star, every atom on every moon

They scribble pretty thoughts in their notepad all day
But our author
Blessed artist that they are
Has yet to add our plot
Our climax
And our ending

443. We're all children
Too short to see above the crowd
So, God helps us see
By putting our spirits on his shoulders

444. God's a child
Who's still quite short, too
So, when he wants, we help him see
By holding him in our arms

445. God is a polyamorous relationship
Between mercury, sulfur, and salt

446. God is the third wheel
At every bar she goes to
Beer in her hand
Silence in her mouth
Knowing she is loved
But not knowing if she's wanted

447. God is lonely
Sitting above
The heavens and the earth
He stares at us
In our snug, loving homes
And wishes he, too
Could live the art of intimacy

448. God holds herself
Because she knows
That the day will come
When she, too, is forgotten
So, she's learning how to love herself
In her own arms

449. God breaks herself apart
And looks at all the pieces
The hate, the wrath
The hope, the healing
She sees her faults
And guides them gently
She feels her strength
And holds it close
To know yourself deeply
Is a gift, a curse
But like a jigsaw puzzle
God mends these broken shards
Piecing them together
Until she is whole again

450. God is staring back at me
From across the living room
Sharing memories, sharing sorrows
Eyes locked, we understand
It's time for our story to meet its end

451. God is the small gesture
When your friend turns to you
And asks, "How are you?"

⚬ ⚬

452. God is
The interpersonal skills
Listed
On your resume

453. 455. God is bitcoin
I kind of get it
I mostly don't

454. God carries no gender
In their weary, resting bones
Simply the salt that feeds
The coarseness of the Earth
A consciousness, a love
For restless seas and gentle waves

455. God is your bangs that you cut in front of your
Bathroom mirror
Such grandeur, for at every moment
You deserve another chance to redefine yourself

⚬ ⚬

456. God slips backward
Into a shining black abyss
Arms spread like a dancer
Fingers stretched
Shoulders taut
Knees bent
Toes pointed

Xe closes xir eyes
And lets xirself fall

457. God lets go
Of absolutely everything
What's above, what's below
Every in and every out
Gone, forever
Cast out into the open sea

458. Every time a door closes
God tries zir best to keep the window open
But lately, the wind demands
It stay shut

459. God is
Constant joy
Never slowing down
Never letting up
Joy! Joy! Joy!

You cannot!
You will not!
Let! It! Stop!

460. God is
A hunger you cannot satisfy
A thirst you cannot quench
A waiting, a tension
A peace, never obtained

461. God is an extra limb you must cut off

462. God cries for her sister
And sinks for her mother
Down the stairs
As they wait
As they pray
For the phone
To finally ring

463. God is
Your lived experience
Right here
Right NOW
You cannot
You must not wait
Until you're punching up daisies
To pull in their fading light

464. God is perfect
Don't you dare say otherwise
I swear I'll eat you alive
If you dare even try

465. God dries out
Like the petals of a rose
Delicate, my dear
They die because they're delicate

466. With a gasp
God casts out a frail hand to the thin wall

467. God includes
Twenty stages of grief
Denial
Anger
Sadness
Boredom
Existential poetry
Nihilism
Optimism
Wrath
Fatter thighs
Skinnier tongues
Bargaining
Stealing
Regret about the stealing
Half-assed art
Full-assed art
Your first lover
Your last lover
Retirement at an age later than you'd like
One final look to the sky
And acceptance

468. God died
Many years ago
Cradled in her mother's arms
She was buried, forgotten
A busy world kept buzzing

But ashes to ashes
Dust to dust
Within the dirt
Honeysuckle flowers
Twist among her bones
And prairie dropseed
Rises from her throat
No spirit is left for us to bow to
But in its place, a garden now grows

469. God
Please do not take note
Of the seltzer water
That I stole
From the basement fridge

I could write ten million poems each day and not even scratch the surface unpacking such a rich spiritual question on what "God" (Or "Light," "Love," "The Universe," whatever you want to call she/they/ze/fae/xi/he/it/etc) truly is.

My perception is limited to my lived experience in the material sense (and, quite frankly, esoteric sense, too). I'm a nonbinary, queer Quaker/spiritualist (?) who started this book in my mid-twenties and ended it in my early thirties who grew up "middle class" (what does that even mean in today's economy?) in the suburbs of Chicago in what is today called the United States but truly is Turtle Island, comes from Irish and Palestinian ancestry and sort of some other European ones, has white skin, was raised Catholic, likes reading and writing (obviously), collects mugs and plants, enjoys boom bap hip-hop music and spiders, hates anything maple flavored, except maple syrup, spent a lot of freetime these past few years unemployed/underemployed while staring at beige ceilings, remains terrified of ovens after I set one on fire by accident, once "thought it was a fart" and got diarrhea right before my first-period orchestra class during my freshman year of high school all while wearing a short skirt, among all sorts of all other things.

Despite my full-hearted belief that all life is connected into a sacred whole, I could never fully encapsulate the vivid tapestry of individual experiences and spiritual awakenings, human or not, no matter how hard I tried.

That's why I invite you, dear reader, to use these blank pages to write (or draw, vomit, whatever) your own thoughts below, exploring what God means to you, what God doesn't mean to you, what God means to you when you're sad, when you're happy, when you're outside and sneeze because of something in the air, when you swear you felt a spider crawling on your skin but it was just a hair, or maybe you don't have hair on your body but still sometimes get that sensation on your skin anyway, or maybe you never have had that sensation no matter whether you have a hairy body, or maybe you've never been around a spider or even know what one looks like.

And so on.

Acknowledgments

A thank you to Alayna, Jocelyn, and Leah, my beta readers, for both their encouragement and editorial support while writing this piece.

A thank you to Shukria, whose mentorship allowed me to open doors I did not even know were there.

A thank you to the Friends Meeting of Washington, whose loving space and enriching community brought my work to the starting line.

Thank you to Eric, Jo, Mareesa, and all the staff at Fernwood Press for getting this book to the finish line.

And the biggest thank-you to my parents. I was in the midst of an incredibly rough life patch during the time period of writing this book. Their unconditional love and support is what kept me going.

www.ingramcontent.com/pod-product-compliance
Lightning Source LLC
LaVergne TN
LVHW030922080826
845145LV00013B/3010

* 9 7 8 1 5 9 4 9 8 2 2 3 1 *